T0064694

In the Quick of Time

In the Quick of Time

Poems

Dru Dougherty

Archway Publishing books may be ordered
through booksellers or by contacting:

Archway Publishing
1663 Liberty Drive
Bloomington, IN 47403
www.archwaypublishing.com
1 (888) 242-5904

Because of the dynamic nature of the Internet, any web
addresses or links contained in this book may have changed
since publication and may no longer be valid. The views
expressed in this work are solely those of the author and do
not necessarily reflect the views of the publisher, and the
publisher hereby disclaims any responsibility for them.

ISBN: 978-1-4808-2770-7 (sc)
ISBN: 978-1-4808-2771-4 (e)

Library of Congress Control Number: 2016902379

Print information available on the last page.

Archway Publishing rev. date: 04/22/2016

For Pituca

"The quivering nimble hour of the present, this is the quick of Time…. The quick of the universe is the *pulsating, carnal self,* mysterious and palpable."

D. H. Lawrence, "The Poetry of the Present"

Contents

The Finer Edge of Ruin 1

I	I'm growing fur	2
II	Just about	3
III	Whitman	4
IV	Time to give up	6
V	My words are not	8
VI	Holdup	10
VII	Blink of an eye	11
VIII	Nude	12
IX	Gray beard	13
X	Seen from afar	14
XI	Stubble trouble	16
XII	Once a week	18

Cascades 19

XIII	Alpine	20
XIV	When *thisorder*	22
XV	Disoriented	24
XVI	Lucretius	26
XVII	Honey	28
XVIII	Stories	30
XIX	It would be so nice	31
XX	… on the high wire	32
XXI	Randy	33

A Sonnet Cycle 35

| XXII | Departure | 36 |

XXIII	*Memento mori*	37
XXIV	Chain Gang	38
XXV	Solstice Birth	39
XXVI	Pronouns	40
XXVII	Coming of Age	41
XXVIII	Arion Rescued from Pirates by a Dolphin	42
XXIX	Proserpina's Promise	43
XXX	Still Alive	44
XXXI	Paquita's Jewel	45
XXXII	The Language of Flowers	46
XXXIII	Mammal Memory	47
XXXIV	*Ars Amatoria*: Touch	48
XXXV	Pollination	49
XXXVI	Self-portrait	50
XXXVII	Orb Web	51
XXXVIII	Country Western	52
XXXIX	St. George's Agony	53
XL	Under Attack	54
XLI	Crystal Orb	55
XLII	An Applied System of Forces that Tends to Strain or Deform a Body	56

State of War 57

XLIII	AK-47	58
XLIV	Sea's up	60
XLV	Witness	61
XLVI	*Action mode*	63
XLVII	Getting	64
XLVIII	Once in a while	66
XLIX	Weather Alert	68

El Tío Antonio...69

L	He mumbles	70
LI	Asleep	71
LII	Slugged, mugged	72
LIII	Forgot	73
LIV	We were there	74

Odds and Evens...75

LV	East Helena	76
LVI	Ice House	79
LVII	A Full Summer Day in Hoyo de Manzanares	81
LVIII	Railroad Spike	83
LIX	Brick Wall	85
LX	Imperfect Sight	87
LXI	Aubade	89

The Finer Edge of Ruin

I

I'm growing fur
some would say a beard
some would say a silver
shield
some an early shroud.
I'm very unsure
it suits me—
so familiar my face
the young face
I'm used to seeing
used to being
and talking to.
So far he's silent
giving it a chance
a month or two
patient with his
doubter
waggish with his
troubled, stubbled
doubled
dru.

II

Just about
end of my rope
at the,
rest of my life
for the
edge of my he-hood
at the

minus
hearing, sex, gall-
bladder, prostate
minus
cronies, job-joy
protean projects
(oh well…)
minus
brain beating brush
in the jungle…

vexed,
hexed
by that
haywire
built-in
out-of-date
out-of-dates
$^{cl}o_{c}{}^{k}{}_{i}$

3

III

Whitman
had one
so did Lincoln
do did
Vincent Van Gogh.
Greats who
led with their
chin—
made poems
paintings
proclamations
stirred
spurred
4   by whiskers
(don't laugh);
solace for fingers
in deep thought
deep trouble—
free the slaves
free the fettered verse
free color and brush
to undo
redo
a found world.

Manic,
talismanic
seers
stroking their
lucky charm.

Three cheers!

IV

Time to give up
give in
shave the rag-tag
scraggle,
quit!
Bums away!

No!

Shabby, yes
but growing its way
to full form—
to
mug hug
ring my maw
cling ever so sweetly
to chin
upper lip
jaw;
like gray mist
half-way up
a thunder cone
like fragile foam
creeping up the sand.

6

Nope,
no white flag for me—
no way!

Patience—
raise the bone
exhume the flesh
shower the would-be
shag
then groom it
ever so gent-
ly,
the way redwoods
comb the clouds.

V

My words are not
my own.
Take *beard*, for
instance.
If only it were mine—
alone
under lock and key
in a drawer
a secret drawer
at home
unknown to Webster
American Heritage
the OED,
you name it.
So intimate
personal
it can't be
simply
beard;
the common word
doesn't do it
doesn't say it
the way it
curls
this way and that
grows
like wanton weed
demands attention
like a little kid
makes a show

of itself
a second self–
anonymous...

Hey-you
'scuseme
whatsyername?

VI

Holdup
masked man
stick 'em up
keep 'em up
gun point
gun barrel
keep yer gold
gimme yer bloom
gimme yer young
groin.

Loner
bandana beard
damndest thing
y'ever saw
y'ever heard
left my wallet
stole my youth
stole my young
unsprung life.

Rode away
him'n it
lickety-split.

VII

Blink of an eye
in time's timeless
mindless
come and go.

Witness
willows
always the aspen
spruce
and pine;
deep pull of runoff
—urgent—
under the fragile
floating
birch-bark
canoe.

Blink.

Take a long look
before the long
bend
before billows, mist
rainbows
before the ground-
less, sight-
less, end-
less
falls—

the river's beard.

VIII

Nude,
the body blessed—
flesh at rest
not final though,
not fired
to oven–ash
urn–ash
not just yet.

Spent
yes!
after
blessed event
loin-join,
night
flesh–mesh
strain! strain!
joy–toy
pro-long
the carnal
song…

Mine thine
thine mine;
couple coupled—
rhyme time!

IX

Gray beard
old fart
Alzheimer's bound;
box-car
up the line
freight weight
not far
dead weight
deadline
boxed in
box in the ground.

Good guy, good
try
hung on
so long
thought ahead
bought ahead;
charge card
ticket
one way
barge way
river sticks
chair-on
sit back…

hell of a view!

X

Seen from afar
battle
scar
the whites of
their eyes
hanging on
hanging off
your jaw.

What war was that?
What wound
from
ear to ear?

Take your pick–
Europe
built 'em best
factory fresh
model '14, '36, '39...
and counting;
then the USA
Korea, Nam, Iraq ...
don't forget the
tribes:
Muslims—Jews
Serbs—Croats
Hutu—Tutsi
Cains—Abels...
more wars
than hairs
on your chinny-chin-chin.

Seen up close
Juan Gris-gray—
a hanky
bandage
blood-stained rag
nose shield
rotted flesh
bodies burned
hide your face
hide your
shame.

Actually,
it's only a beard
left behind
in a trench.

XI

For Michael Iarocci

Stubble trouble—
the why
the wherefore
me 'n it
cheek by jowl,
some kind of sign
for what?

So you're
getting along
in years
sixty-nine-time
so what?
So you're
scared-stiff
dead-end
ain't no more
so what?
You and every-
body
over the hill
past your prime
ah!
but you
dear dru
odd
fellow-fellow
let your whiskers

grow
(while
bone and flesh
wane to
naught
nil)
so you can
calibrate
articulate
celebrate

your ruin.

XII

Once a week
you trim
the gray badge
of ruin
rushing toward collapse
on your chin.

Seven milli-
meters over all,
two at neck
five at jaw;
preen dream
this blade machine
hand-held
guillotine
the fur fury
the hair hurry
growing-growing
to bury hairy!

Once a week
mister whisker
exercises
mowing-mowing
the overgrowing
wreath
on his chin.

Cascades

XIII

Alpine
stream beam
drop by drop
cascades
on nipple-nape
down
spinal gorge to
bangle balls
or tingle-tangle wet
triangle
to live arms
and drippled legs
to sweet feet
20 wading in warm
dream-steam!

Yes!
our hyper
unfurred
proto-mammal skin,
bare to pluvi-air
(tryst mist)
to indoor
spatter-chatter
Yes! Yes!
our
daily
hydro pleasure
naked epidermi-
treasure—

welcome male fe-
male
bi- or trans-
to our wistful
blissful

    H   W   R
S   O   E

     O   R
  H   U   !

       .

      . . .

    . . . . .

   . . . .

  . . . .

 . . . .

XIV

When *thisorder*
(what we take for granted
as order)
gives way to dis – order
you suddenly know
how comfortable
how desirable
thisorder was.

It supplied a reason
to be
hungry useful funny
et cetera,
it allowed memory to
wea_ken without embarrassment
and let wildness
linger in disguise,
oh, yes
thisorder was a friend
to the end
to the very last bend
in the river
before the delta

before
current divides
and helter-skelter
wanders here and there
s l o w s
goes every which way,

a wet snake
lost in its meanders
on the border
of pure dis – order:
restless motion
(the ancient ocean)
where mighty rivers
≈Amazon Mekong
Columbia and Mississippi
Ganges Euphrates
the Volga the Nile≈
all rush
to
d

   .

  1

e

XV

.

.

.

Disoriented
lost my East
misplaced it
somewhere
no dawn today
for me
careless of you
dru!
woke up
and it was gone
just like that
maybe in the
trunk
of the car?
under the doormat?
behind the
davenport?

I miss my East
so bright
first light
behind the hills
every day
a fresh start,
a new Alpha…

The birds are gone
too…

East,
where the hell
are you?

XVI

Lucretius
woke up
looked up
cooked up
the Cosmos.

Good gracious!

There is, there are
atoms
emptiness
motion,
no more
no less.

He lay in bed
awed by
simplicity—
atoms
make matter
(his bladder for instance)
they move
through the void
(like his bowels
after breakfast...)

Voilà
the nature of
Nature
every thing

every creature!
Hunger stirred
but wonder won
his reason spun:
motion =
change
and change =
death,
the matter-scatter
atoms disperse
your brain
your breath
your life
a rainbow after rain
that dims
fades
so something new
a seed, a weed
can form
be born
a
part of you
Atom–Adam
in it.

He rose
relieved himself
watched his yellow arc
give back
its warm spark
to the ground
of
everything.

XVII

"Honey"
that's what my dad
called my mom
when they were good.

Honey
not in a hive
not in a jar
not bought

made
when ripe berries
picked on a farm
turned to jam
when she told us kids
"sleep outside on the quilts
and count the shooting stars
tonight"
what a sight!
And when she cut my toast
into strips
and spread the dulcet jam
while I, abed
lay meager
with fever.

"Honey"
dropped out of sight
and sound
in the 60s

when all went wrong—
days of ash and gall
when Jack, Bobby and Martin
lost the light
when mom and dad
split
each to their own
night

bitter
unsweet
unsung

till now.

XVIII

Stories
promise a there-
fore
a what-
for
an arrow
flying to score
a bull's-eye;
but this
poor
stuttering thing
broken string
literary ding-a-ling
does nothing
goes nowhere
on its way to
undo
the who
the others expect to
find
not a
hidden
one of a kind
not me
not thee.
Us!

XIX

It would be so nice
just to go home
and be alone…

no one to ask
where I've been
what I've done
no one…

every inch
of every room
just the way I
left it
the way I
like it—
undisturbed

no chitchat
no TV
only me
myself and I
alone
at home
content
all three
(for a while
or two).

XX

For Pose and Mary

… on the high wire
no net below
in real time
between eternities
take a step
inhale the future
another step
exhale the past
pulse, no pause
go, go
breath, no pause
now, now
in the quick of time
step a step
no net below
go, go …

XXI

Randy
handy dandy
autumn leaves ablaze
late fits of craze.
So?
whadja expect?

Anyhow
it's all in your head
(the sexual organ *sans
pareille
n'est pas?*)

out to pasture
age-rage
memories of rapture
still in the
blood.
No! *Stilled*
tamed by statins
maimed by pharma-hawkers'
beta blockers...

Forget it
accept it, man
the race is
all
but run
the finish line
up ahead

(this isn't only
in your head)

· · · · · · · · · · · · · · ·

whozat guy
limping
aching
left in his
own
lust-dust?

A Sonnet Cycle

XXII Departure

A blind alley at midday—all gloom,
Fire escapes, dumpsters, maybe a bum
Laid out in the shadows—immobile, numb
Exile from life's double-crossing loom.

A passing glance, enough to spur stride, feel
Hormone hit the vein, hackles rise.
All unconscious, of course, coward but wise,
Tutored by sage glands that fear unseal.

Flee! Flee! But you stop, return, breast
The breakers on the dim concrete beach,
Step over garbage, eye the ugly breach
Unbrave, unsure on what myopic quest.

One-way shaft to nowhere, unmapped, unknown.
Without a thought—that least!—into the zone.

36

XXIII *Memento mori*

The crown dies first on a Douglas fir.
The lifeless snag is born top-down,
Descending year after year, air to ground,
Birthed its death in a gentle, green blur.

Cairn of the living tree—spar-spur
Stripped of sail, bare bleached horn
Broke by thunder, by rain-sheet torn.
On its jags, cougar and grizzly leave their fur.

Granite gray from dawn to dusk, the snag
Unmossed, unboughed, is froze in final gawk.
Where green-sweep once mocked the mute crag,

See ghost post, where eagle, hawk
And raven—gold, rust and somber flags—
Fly their colors, and hikers stay their talk.

XXIV Chain Gang

For Milton Azevedo

Penguins march seventy miles to lay
An egg, go hungry for months—three!—
To keep a single yoke warm, and stay
Standing in timeless night, longing for the sea.

An heroic march! Bird and winter locked
In fettered feud, love to duty chained.
But, no! In fact absurdly joined, the flock
Pacing on ice as DNA ordained.

Step… step… the birds that swim repeat
38   The epic march, refrain of a refrain, ordered
By mindless need mapped by feathered feet.
Retraced the single course their genes recorded.

Emperors, who leave the deep only to mate,
Wherewith the wings to flee your frozen fate?

XXV Solstice Birth

Nigh the horizon, it looms angry and red
As giant Jupiter. Our solitary moon, suspended
In black—to us, blue—space, the upended
Daughter, just from the womb, whose crowned head

Burst into view a long memory ago,
Her face as dark and scarlet as the lone orb.
Nostrils cleared, for hunger's blood to absorb
The planet's air, she cries, lets go

Crimson placenta and takes first breath.
Woman giving birth to woman, yells
Of pain and joy, a cord whose knowing cells
Bind us all to mother, and to matter's death:

The full moon, ascended, shines a borrowed light
On mammals less alone this darkest night.

XXVI Pronouns

Vivir en los pronombres
To live in pronouns
Pedro Salinas, *La voz a ti debida*

If light can be particle be wave be both
At the same time, why don't we love we hate
As poets warned eons ago, our bonded mate
Despite the promise pledge of marriage oath?

If atoms spin right spin left are here are there
As quantum theory says, why can't we wine
Taste—sun soil the very vine—
And think the sense those flavors bare?

We can we do, naturally. What else is new
Under this ripening star? Dilemma's horns,
Oxymoron's frigid fire, the is 'n isn't of metaphor

Tell us we're twins, triplets, quads, quins, more
Than we know, want to know, since being born
Since you and I, he and she, make us make you.

XXVII Coming of Age

A prophesy writ in hair and swelling flesh
Bleeding by the moon. Yet no journey, oracle, riddle.
Announce what? Decipher what? In that fresh
Body, future is past, beauty its own sibyl.

A legacy handed down in blood and cell
Willed by a matriarch lost to memory, her task
Completed, its treasure sealed in skin that tells
Her tale and, therein, her fertile destiny forecasts.

Awakening in her own river, pushed by currents
Risen in runoff, eager for rapids' spray,
Deep sovereign channel, and lazy rich

Delta. All this foretold without seer or witch,
Copied in breasts and hips, the unsigned clay
That soft marble divines—jubilant, exuberant!

XXVIII Arion Rescued from Pirates by a Dolphin

Herodotus (I. 23)

> The morning's miracle, hard as rock,
> The pulse pounding in warm sheets
> That wrap this mummy against the shock
> Of autumn air, arisen, my stirring greets.
> Was I reborn when the cock
> Crowed, pecking at the dawn with beet-
> Red comb? Or was it the body's clock
> Whetted and abetted the feral feat?
>
> For answer I turned to sage mate
> Who, nudged and gently plied,
> Solved the crux, baring her bait
> To which this Arion rose, astride
> A dolphin who bore him straight
> To port, resurrecting his human hide.

42

XXIX Proserpina's Promise

For Luis Murillo

This year the side meadow is indelibly lush.
The grass, wildflowers, even the brush
By the stone fence seem kin to the rose.
Waist deep I stand in blossom, my nose
A canvass in a field of lilac and first
Lilies, honeysuckle, mint; my thirst
For new color whetted by bluebells,
Yellow bells, minute daisies, villanelles
Written by the goddess to keep her twin pledge:
"I will return," she said, at Earth's far edge
Whose dim netherworld—grim half
Of the whole—she entered a maid. Her autograph[43]
Is present in this field I parse, loath to budge
Lest her hand—*florida*—these feet besmudge.

XXX Still Alive

Siempre, siempre silvestre
Always, always wild
Jorge Guillén, "Naturaleza viva"

When the afternoon sun clears the south gable
And bathes breathing wood, its rich grain
Plays a fugue of color and whorls, each vein
A map of cherry pit become a table.

Standing on delicate legs, the polished planks
Defy the first death of log and limb,
Gleaming an aura that felling couldn't dim:
The sheen of river bark on wooded banks.

44

Each narrow slat, glued and gently doweled
To be raised again, with nerves of timbered lace,
Draws its signature for eye and hand to trace:
No epitaph, this, for a tree disemboweled

But autograph of wild sapling wood
Still standing, as no human ever could.

XXXI Paquita's Jewel

A ring of rubies and diamonds set in gold—
A single row of gems gracing her old
Wrinkled finger, shining like eyes she recalled
From sixty years before, washed and hauled
From the dirt of memory, love's rich mine.
A gift of friend or suitor, on that she declined
To say from whom and why: a pact
With silence, a show of faith to his act
Of pledging a future, in stones professed,
Brilliant as his manicured nails that pressed
The band to bone, still unbent, uncold.
A jeweled portal to past affection, a bold
Regress to years long forgot, to desire
Still warm in faithful rubies flanked by fire.   45

XXXII The Language of Flowers

Alcea rosea, the humble hollyhock,
Graced the alley that divided their block.
Much-much too hokey for affluent lawns,
Unfit to mingle with faux metal fawns.

Hear a neon bell, a purple horn, a pink
And white trumpet: totally out of sync
With daffodils, roses, potted palms—pride
Of fashionable gardens on the wealthy West Side.

Gangly, awkward, they grew like adolescents,
The fuzz on their stems intimating pubescence.
Swaying in the wind on overgrown stalks,
Boogie-woogie bloomed on common hollyhocks.

Too awkward, too plain, they were deemed
                                    [lowbred:
So back by the alley where the trash-men tread.

XXXIII Mammal Memory

Mais où son les neiges d'antan?
Where are the snows of yesteryear?
François Villon, "Ballade des dames du
temps jadis"

They melted. Time's impassive torch saw to that.
But ancient passions flicker, then flame at the least
Whiff of scent, the briefest flash of flat
Belly between sweats… puffs to wake the beast!

Too stubborn to expire, too rooted to run,
They stay put, swaying in restless air,
Tired trees fraught with decay, undone
But unfinished; tinder liable to catch and flare.

47

Dreams are worst. Nets for memories that feel
Exactly as they felt before bursting carapace
And dying in time's trap: the moths' ordeal,
Insensate—wings spread—pinned in a case.

What sun can wither desire? What wind can break
Its back? This mammal remembers, dreaming
                                        [awake.

XXXIV *Ars Amatoria*: Touch

In dreams you touch a woman's naked thigh.
Her wetness waits, blushed by frank desire.
Your hand lingers on the warm silk, the high
Curve of satin flesh. Your fingers never tire.

But she does. Unlike wine, lust is pure haste,
More urgent than love, untutored to savor and wait.
Over anxious to arrive, it skitters by chaste
caress, to gratify our genes' genius: Replicate!

The sense of senses, waked by our mother's skin,
Instructed by her nipple, neck, maternal heat.
Making love, the newborn gets to nestle again,
And sex is less to sire than relish and repeat.

In dreams, we lose the past and future tense.
In bed, delay and silk redress our sense.

XXXV Pollination

Count four rows of petals, a lush
Symmetry of flower flesh, a pink star
In its own green cosmos. Dead center, a blush
Of intense red, bursting from a white scar

Of stamens tipped with pollen packs—a Renoir
Hue. The tree has a dozen living lights
Flashing "welcome" in the air—an opulent pulsar
Hung to advertise Eden to Fancy's flight.

Camille, Camilla, Camelia, untold delights,
Attract the shy Armand, cruelly charmed
By the lip-like furls of the corolla, sights
Irresistible to any nectar-nosing bee. Disarmed   49

By the soft garland and the ruddy promise of scent,
Hell-bent into Heaven's sticky stigma, he went.

XXXVI Self-portrait

Hooded eyelids, a slow hazel stare
Under a Teton brow. Curly gray hair,
A fleshy nose, prominent jaw and chin,
A flash of gold—no guile—in a ready grin.

Bow-tied at work, slippers and fleece at home,
He rises early, eager to tweak his tome.
Scholar by day, a wayward rebel at night,
Of techy gizmos, a hopeless neophyte.

Unfriend to Church, ever faithful to the clan,
His "howdy" and "toodle-oo" mark a modest man.
Outward, calm as crust; inward tense
50   As buried faults waiting to thrust. Hence,

What he seems to be, he both is and ain't.
A faithful likeness, yes, but… it's only paint.

XXXVII Orb Web

A spider web designed to trap, each thread
Spun to parallel, loop-around and tug,
So common airy things become a snug
Wrap, a holy tomb, a Pharaoh's bed.

Head-down in hunger's artful void,
The patient spinner hangs, surveying, at rest,
His fatal orb. Master maker of viscoid
Lines, he dangles, waiting for his dinner guest.

A risky throw of life's dice! Luck
May tangle a lizard's tongue in beauty's net
Turning hunter, in his own snare stuck,

To prey. But isn't risk the parasite of any bet?
The maker of silky filaments puts his buck
On feasting (and art), so he too may beget.

XXXVIII Country Western

They were two, and heaps more before 'em,
Made one in rut clutch, huff and puff,
A cocked canon balled with beer, enough
To twine orgastic yells: life's ¡*crème de la crème*!

Cow-hand, cow-girl, twain jeans in a country bar:
Week-end wassail, the usual raunchy romp.
"You dance, cowboy?"
                    "You becha; let's tromp!"
And that they did, to banjo, fiddle and steel guitar.

See Jack: boots, silver buckle, new rodeo vest.
See Jill: blonded braids and Teton bust
52 Bustin' pearl buttons on her checkered shirt.

"Let's skedaddle, gal."
                    "I'll just git my quirt."
They both rode saddle on ole buckin' lust,
Meanest mornin-after bronc in the windy West.

XXXIX St. George's Agony

Perpetual penumbra, shutters drawn
Against Satan's glare; wind airborne
By witless fans: nurses, nuns, saw-
Bones spurn his battle lust and scorn.

Memories wasting for lush lawns
Scarred by fresh-shod hooves, for helmet dewed
And lady's saffron scarf; for armor brawn.
Idle pike and blade his fey fists reprove.

Agony's unnatural shade, hospital flaws
Void of fame prized by loyal retinue
witness to honor, to hand-like claws,
To flames and wings the plated demon flew.

In a private room a TV spews, unraw
Unreal, to numb the one who dragons slew.

XL Under Attack

Give her a castle. Give her a granite keep
For that fragile flower. No more sheet-rock,
Hollow doors, walls of cinder block.
Build her ramparts and a moat, oceans deep.

Two words can twenty arrows be, shot
At a frightened rose. A question can cut as true
As tempered steel. A mere look may undo
The cherry bloom, its chaste blossom rot.

Lilacs, sweet-peas, night-blooming jasmine,
To the tower! You're under siege by a timeless, genetic
Power, who would conquer with ax and mail.

54

Love—and flee—thine enemy! Hemmed in,
You, too, would woo the wind with pathetic
Plea to subdue. Turn no cheek. Countervail!

XLI Crystal Orb

As from a thousand prisms
Shelley, "Epipsychidion"

On your open palm, a clear crystal sphere
Throbbing with light; the transparent stream
Shatters—flocks of frenzied parrots appear!
Translucent matter, inert till errant beams

Enter and seek its flaw—original dirt—
Blade where chaste waves fall and scream.
The orb is mute till spectra, bled but unhurt,
Cascade into view—an Impressionist painter's
[dream!

No Merlin is at work, no knight cased in mail,
But magic, still. When the sun-rays bleed
From cell to cell in their prism jail,
Watch colors spook, rear and stampede.

Impure crystal, arcane ax that drips,
Hidden rainbows—wonders—at our fingertips!

XLII An Applied System of Forces that Tends to Strain or Deform a Body

Tension (now called stress) is everywhere
Stretched to the limit, like a promise about to break,
Or trust unattended, frayed, in disrepair.
New-born to grizzled geezer: pains and aches.

Whence the strain? It's not just you and me—
We hapless mammals. Think the planet's plates
Grinding into or lava-lathering the bed of seas;
Think storm-winds whirling, clouds gyrating

56

Till funnel-tunnel touches and maims. You breathe
Their air and walk faults on a thin crust
Afloat on a fiery moat. Mother Earth

Oblivious to tsunamis, blind and deaf to seethe
With anger, crush marble to dust, up-thrust
That first life-or-death breath—your birth!

State of War

XLIII AK-47

a gun
(a dumb thing, heavier
than handwriting)
Velimir Khlebnikov, "Bad News"

We know who designed this thing:
Mijail Kalashnikov (retired General).
And we know when: 1941
shortly after the Nazi invasion
of the old USSR.
It was, and still is,
a marvel in its class—
600 rounds a minute,
operational submerged in water,
mud, sand, snow;
light-weight, only nine parts
easy to assemble;
currently in use by Armed Forces
in over fifty countries.

The bottom line:
more than
100,000,000 units
sold since creation.
The US M-16
can't touch it.
It sells for only $235.

Anywhere there's a war, a military action,
a peace-keeping presence,
the AK-47 is there.

Our associates are standing by
to receive your call.

Please have a credit card handy.

XLIV

Sea's up
man's down
deck's awash
man'll drown
'lessen rope
sure as Hell
'lessen hope
take it, tie it
round his chest
round his guts
Move it!

Man's down
sea's up
crack 'a dawn
he's hangin' on
get him
don't let him...
Watch it!

XLV Witness

I wake and feel the fell of dark, not day...
Gerard Manley Hopkins

Hecatomb, holocaust. Ugly words,
dark words lit by all burning in the bones built,
the bones broke and flesh unfilled.

Où sont les Shoshones d'antan,
les doux et pacifiques Shoshones?

Homicida, homicidium. The beast butcher,
scour blood brimmed
lest bitter we taste, lest stain remain.

Où sont les Pieds Noires d'antan,
les hautaines Pieds Noires?

Ravage, ruin. Disembowel the foul,
truss their fell, dress their scourge,
trophy horn and hide.

Où sont les Têtes–Plates d'antan,
les beaux Têtes–Plates?

World-wake. Trumpets crash,
Banished to *oblivio*, to ash &
non esse. Trash, this page too.

Où sont les Sioux, les Kootenai, les Gros Ventres,
les Cheyennes, les féroces Crow d'antan?

XLVI

Action mode —
two words
like
two boots
marching off
to war.

Kill or
be killed
for what
for whom?

For
whose what
and
whose whom?

Two words
stamping off
to war

against war.

XLVII

Getting
so used to
war

the hawk talk
of
smart bombs,
IEDs,
the godlike
drone strike…

The wars
are always with us

remember Nam?
remember the MiG-15s at
the 38th Parallel?
remember the Bay of Pigs,
Operation *Limpieza* in
Santo Domingo
the invasion of Grenada
(condemned by the UN)?
remember the Gulf War
Operation *Infinite Reach*
the bombing of Bagdad
and
our longest-ever war,
Afghanistan.

Getting so used
to wars
or is it
one long war
we're in,
the war on peace

that no one can win?

XLVIII

Once in a while
the cosmos gives us
a white buffalo;
it's a rare event
scary for some
sacred for others;
a comet
with hair and horns
a portent to ask
why?
what went wrong?
how long
will it take?

Once in a blue moon
the furry calf
drops to Earth
in its translucent sac
a four-leggëd ghost
cousin to fresh
snow
and bleached bones.

It, too, has a mother
feeds, craps
frisks
under the big sky
unprotected, unarmed
but for flinty hooves
obsidian horns

and the herd
once free
now subdued.

Where a white buffalo
dies
crocus, butter cups
and shooting stars
bloom year round.

XLIX Weather Alert

A cleft between clouds, figures hugging mud walls
To escape the raid; dry sycamore leaves
Rattling in the haze. The first lightning bolt cleaves
The wind. Then rain—dark as oil—scrawls
Its signature on earth. A brief notice, followed
By indiscriminate hell, chill, a paralyzing
Burst that deafens and blinds. Thunder equalizing
Grief. Even sheltered, all could be swallowed.

Terror first fell from clouds, blameless, pointless,
Redolent of ozone and sulfur. From the cruel cleft
Bolts never-ending, unpredictable, zig-zagging
From thunderhead to dust, at each checkpoint less
Human, uncontainable, until nothing's left
But charred metal or flesh: no malice, no fragging.

El Tío Antonio

L

He mumbles
words crumble
in his mouth.

Antonio
háblame claro,
¡coño!

No speech,
instead
the sound
of an ocean
receding
retreating
down a beach.

Antonio
talk to me
damn it!

LI

Asleep
present
but absent

skin and
bones
under
the sheet.

Give me
your hand
old man
your cold
fist
your anger
something
anything
I can hold.

LII

Slugged, mugged
not by hoodlums
by life instead.

Antonio!

tied to your bed
out of your head
you frighten me;
gone south
a stranger
a danger to yourself.

72   Drugged, thugged,
end of the
man-man

Antonio, come back!

LIII

Forgot
left to rot
tied to his chair
to his blank stare.

Antonio Gutiérrez
Maestro del billar
caged
aged 96
fed, washed
treated like a babe
a very bored
babe
holding on to life
holding on to rage.

His hand, my hand
our eyes
nothing said
only a half-smile
a knowing nod
instead.

Antonio Gutiérrez
farewell.

LIV

We were there,
Tío

your niece
weeping
your Yankee friend
keeping the faith.

We were there
at the window

when the piston
pushed your coffin
into the
fire
into the gyre
those dry pegs
your
death-camp
arms and legs.

On the way out
they gave us two seedlings
of an oak.

Odds and Evens

LV East Helena

A G ⊤ H E
  L   .   A
S   .   P
     .
     .
     .

Torrid lava tongue
down
clinker
crag
down
cinder
slope

nothing precious—
mineral swill.

A railroad car
a furnace car

        r   c
    i   l
    c   e
    a   k
    t   c
      r   a

    t   d
      i   r
      p   i
        s   p
          s
          .
          .
          .
          .
          .
          .
          .
          .
          .
          .
          .

Molten Metals
z
  i
    g
      a
    n
  d
z
  a
    g

Freezing f
        i
          r
            e

               Smelter s
                  l
                a
             g
            !
          !
        !
      !
    !

LVI Ice House

Maybe the old fridge gave out again,
or mother was making a double batch
of ice-cream. How does one begin

to remember? All I can vaguely snatch
from memory is the ride downtown
to the ice house, a place I attach

to a block of light coming down
a ramp of runners, and then tongs,
black and pointed, a rusted crown

for the translucent wonder that belongs
to winter, frozen lakes and skating rinks.
Not to July's picnics and patriotic songs.

Cold and radiant, the block sinks
into my childhood as I watch it rise
between jaws that **clink! clink!**

before thrusting iron knives
into its smooth, veined sides.
Onto the truck-bed, and dad drives

us home. In sawdust the ice rides
already melting under my arm
that hugs and heats its wounded hide.

Futile. Nothing could stay the harm…
Half melted, when we got to the farm.

LVII A Full Summer Day in Hoyo de Manzanares

For Ignacio Navarrete

Semi-dark, semi-light; a canvas barks,
the curtain crows—it's the day's dawn-yawn.

Sun-up. Shadows elllllllongate hawthorn trees;
rock walls zip one field to the next.

In the meadow a day-old colt, all legs
under his mare—stacking-tables with tails.

The drone of bumble-bees lacing the lavender—
purple pin cushion, black and yellow buttons.

Binary birds dive-bomb feral cats
scattering leaflets—*"This is Magpie Country!"*

The church bell in the village: chime...chime...
swallows dip\dodge incoming time...time...

Noon. Lizards tickle the boulders' shoulders;
eagles draw circles, daisies mime the sun.

An uppity breeze cools the beaded brow;
sprites are about, shaking languid leaves.

Siesta time. Bird-song off, bug-buzz on;
the price of shade triples by the hour.

Dusk raises its parasol. Ladies and bats
through lanes and lofty lawns will stroll.

Crickets and cow-bells; the evening vibrates
in pocket and pulse—unidentified cosmic call.

Venus, then the moon's thin grin. A shooting star
(night's needle) pricks the black balloon.

LVIII Railroad Spike

…it was the age of steam
Seamus Heaney, "Shelf Life"

A rusted railroad spike—
it serves as a paper weight but holds down
lighter heft, like
memories of a clan, a town,
a grandfather who let his family down.

What lies inert on the desk
took years to work itself loose,
rebellious, picaresque
as a red caboose,
or a boxcar-bum's "Let's vamoose."   83

He limped, I walked, the rails
and when I found one, free of its tie,
a black, oily nail
huge in my hand, I'd spy
a wink in his hooded, bloodshot eyes.

We'd take our trophy back
to the workbench in the garage, a place
of refuge, a dreamer's shack,
where it was no disgrace
to drink and cuss, and show his face.

On my last visit
I chose a tapered point from the pile,
its ferrous fire exquisite,
to hold again with infantile
collusion aloft—a grandson's wish to reconcile

Devotion with others' pain.
A thorn, a nail, a pike, a metal spear
that finally split his brain,
wounding everyone near
but me. Our spike, love's dark souvenir.

LIX Brick Wall

Old bricks, salvaged from different sites
to judge from the mix of hues—
ferric red to wild pink to blackened rose
smudged here and there with tints of ash.
A few look chipped, others skewed,
but most lie straight and true.

It's a weight-bearing wall,
holding up the roof of a new saloon
where strangers and couples talk and drink,
often unaware.
Measured ladders of fired earth
rise to a tangle of timbers
hatched by golden bands at sunset.
Take a closer look:
ancient beams hewn with axes;
some are scarred and twisted.

No one seems to notice the wall.
They're too intent on pulse and eyes,
framed by molded mud,
to weigh its premise—
that the past can be retrieved
and then rearranged
in rows of recycled ruin.

Our local lexicon of loss,
in ordered lines that set a classic beat,
indifferent in their plumb
it first appears,
as friends greet and hug
or press a reaching hand
beside its solid plane.

Domed by discarded beams,
laughter rebounds off bricks
tempered in flames long ago
then laid in mortar, just so;
hard-set bricks
that were severed
from their site,
scattered, dumped and
    later
rescued, happily,
for this.
        Cheers!

LX Imperfect Sight

What's lightly hid…
Richard Wilbur, "Ceremony"

Myopia is a gift at Christmastide.
After we trim the tree—the angel alongside
A Santa descending from heaven by parachute,
Profaning holy feathers with fake fur—
I remove my glasses, vision's over-boot,
To appreciate the blur.

My opium is not seeing straight.
I know it's a tree—each ornament ornate
As a Tiffany jewel, or so nostalgia judges—
But in my willing blindness, stripped of specs,   87
I see a triangle lit by smudges
Of multi-colored flecks.

Detail hides the ceremony's secret.
Each different decoration, every precise orbit
Of light—unmixed—sharply defined
In full view with glasses on,
Obscures the vague, unsigned
Sine qua non.

Bring on the eggnog and carols!
'Tis the season to give (and take... of Napa's barrels).
Hurrah for dim, deficient sight!
As I blink, cheaters set aside,
Nebulae grace this nether night—
Supernal to the bleary-eyed.

LXI Aubade

I lie awake night after night
And never get the answers right.
W.B. Yeats, "The Man and the Echo"

Every morning at five o'clock, I open my eyes
And wait. The body is busy checking—heart rate,
Blood pressure, muscle ache, polyps, the size

And state of skin spots, the works! Wide awake,
I wonder how it knows to rouse itself. Sub-surface
                                        [trials
Across some inner fault, perhaps a minor quake?

I'm grateful—better self-checks than self-denials [89]
At any hour—but always puzzled by the sure
Savvy of flesh and blood. What finger lifts and
                                        [dials?

Who sets the clock? Was I born with a chip? So
                                        [obscure
A vigil, is it proof I have a soul? Does this fleshy
                                        [flux
Harbor a deeper, wiser me? Perhaps a Puck to
                                        [assure

Safe passage from five to five o-three. A crux
Worthy of death-bed confusion and midnight's
                                    [dread
Of Nothing, that's nowhere and endless. Shucks,

All I hear is my wife's deep breathing in bed,
The rain tapping at the skylight, drop-drop,
Trains carrying freight to Frisco, then overhead

An airplane's descending whine (not the clop-clop
Of hooves heard by Delmore in his naked cave).
All systems go, I toss till –huh?– the familiar plop

Of the morning paper, sign it's time to shave,
Brew coffee, eat bran flakes, read
90   Yesterday's disasters, idiotic editorials, grave

Predictions of endings by seers of every creed...
Not now. Time for trousers, bowtie, Irish tweed.

Printed in the United States
By Bookmasters